SOCIAL WORK AND CRIMINAL JUSTICE:

VOLUME 3

THE NATIONAL AND LOCAL CONTEXT OF POLICY IMPLEMENTATION

Louise Brown

Liz Levy

The Scottish Office Central Research Unit

and

Gill McIvor

Social Work Research Centre
Department of Applied Social Science
University of Stirling

THE SCOTTISH OFFICE CENTRAL RESEARCH UNIT
1998

ACKNOWLEDGEMENTS

We are indebted to all those who kindly sacrificed a considerable amount of time out of their busy schedules to provide the researchers with their views: representatives of the Main Consultation Group; social work managers; and independent sector providers.

Our thanks are also extended to Pam Lavery and Trish Hughes of the Social Work Research Centre for transcribing taped interviews and to Mrs Helen Pinkman and Ms Mariane McGowan of the Central Research Unit, for their patience in deciphering and typing the various drafts of the report.

Louise Brown
Liz Levy
Gill McIvor
1998

SOCIAL WORK AND CRIMINAL JUSTICE RESEARCH PROGRAMME REPORTS

Paterson, F. and Tombs, J. (1998) — **Social Work and Criminal Justice: Volume 1 - *The Impact of Policy*.** The Stationery Office.

Phase One:

McAra, L. (1998) — **Social Work and Criminal Justice: Volume 2 - *Early Arrangements*.** The Stationery Office.

Phase Two:

Brown, L., Levy, L. and McIvor, G. (1998) — **Social Work and Criminal Justice: Volume 3 - *The National and Local Context*.** The Stationery Office.

Brown, L., Levy, L. (1998) — **Social Work and Criminal Justice: Volume 4 - *Sentencer Decision Making*.** The Stationery Office.

McAra, L. (1998a) — **Social Work and Criminal Justice: Volume 5 - *Parole Board Decision Making*.** The Stationery Office.

McIvor, G. and Barry, M. (1998) — **Social Work and Criminal Justice: Volume 6 - *Probation*.** The Stationery Office.

McIvor, G. and Barry, M. (1998a) — **Social Work and Criminal Justice: Volume 7 - *Community Based Throughcare*.** The Stationery Office.

CONTENTS

SUMMARY

INTRODUCTION

The Policy

In Scotland, statutory social work services to offenders and their families are provided by the local authority social work departments. Since April 1991, the Scottish Office has reimbursed to social work departments the full costs of providing a range of statutory social work services in the criminal justice system. National Objectives and Standards (the National Standards) were introduced by the Social Work Services Group of the Scottish Office to coincide with the introduction of the funding initiative.

The National Standards and the funding initiative cover: social enquiry reports; court social work services; probation; community service; and throughcare (social work in prisons is funded by the Scottish Prison Service). Since 1991, the initiative has been extended to supervised release orders, bail information and accommodation schemes, and supervised attendance order schemes (the latter two schemes are not yet available on a national basis).

The main aims of the Government's policy are:

- to reduce the use of custody by increasing the availability, improving the quality and targeting the use of community based court disposals and throughcare services on those most at risk of custody, especially young adult repeat offenders;
- to enable offenders to address their offending behaviour and make a successful adjustment to law abiding life.

Background to the Research

Central Government's review and evaluation of implementation of the funding initiative and the National Standards involves a programme of inspection by Social Work Services Inspectorate (SWSI), interpretation of statistics and a programme of research.

The research programme examines progress towards policy objectives. Four sheriff court areas each in separate social work authorities, were selected as study sites for Phase Two of the research programme to reflect areas of both high and low population density and to represent both specialist and more generic forms of organising social work criminal justice services. The names of the four areas have been anonymised in reports and are referred to as Scott, Wallace, Burns and Bruce.

This study describes the national and local context within which the policy was developed, implemented and reviewed prior to and during the period in which the research programme was conducted. Findings are based on an analysis of central and local government policy and planning documents, and interviews in spring 1995 with five members of the Main Consultation Group on Social Work Services to the Criminal Justice System; twelve social work managers; and seven independent sector service providers.

CONSULTATION

National consultation, which is conducted primarily through the Main Consultation Group, was generally seen by those members interviewed to have been effective in involving key stakeholders in developing the National Standards and generating a sense of ownership of them.

Some Main Consultation Group interviewees suggested that the Group could have approached the judiciary for more assistance in raising awareness of policy implementation and in the pursuit of a more coherent judicial response to the development of services. At the local level, interviews with sheriffs and social work managers indicated that formal liaison with the judiciary did not always take place in all of the study areas and where this existed, it was not always effective. Informal liaison, in particular between sheriffs and court social workers, was viewed by them to be operating well.

Some Main Consultation Group respondents considered that the proposed inclusion of diversion within 100 per cent funding had given impetus to the development of links with procurators fiscal and to the development of more coherent systems for interacting with court agencies. Managers and those procurators fiscal who were interviewed considered that existing liaison arrangements were satisfactory.

At the national level, liaison between SPS and social work criminal justice services could, some Main Consultation Group representatives believed, be more effective. In addition they indicated that liaison between community based and prison based social workers could be improved.

At the national level, networks between local authorities and the independent sector could, some Main Consultation Group members believed, have been exploited to a greater extent. However, at the local level, social work managers and independent sector providers in the study areas considered that, in general, the nature and extent of liaison had been adequate. They also considered that the National Standards had facilitated good liaison arrangements which resulted in greater accountability.

PLANNING AND FUNDING

Planning

The planning process was believed by managers to have contributed positively to the development of services by providing a focus for the development of services and establishment of priorities within an overall objective. However, interviewees and documents reported that the preliminary planning procedures, introduced at a national level, did not operate effectively at the local level and that absence of reliable statistical information at both the national and local levels hindered strategic planning. Steps have been taken to remedy these problems: revised planning procedures have been introduced and the system for providing national information has been reviewed.

Managers, sheriffs and social workers identified a need for a wider range of specialist services and an increased quantity of available places. Interviewees reported that rural areas experienced particular difficulties in accessing or providing services. Main Consultation Group respondents and managers believed that a more collaborative approach to providing and developing services would be required with smaller authorities following local government reorganisation as smaller authorities would be unable on their own to offer a comprehensive range of services because of diseconomies of scale. This, managers believed, might discourage the independent sector from providing services to smaller, predominantly rural, authorities. Sheriffs were concerned that the full range of services might not be available which would limit the options in each case and the risk of custody might thus become greater.

Funding

Managers and local authority plans expressed concern about obtaining an appropriate level of funding to develop existing services, establish additional specialist services and introduce more innovative methods of work. Managers believed that a comprehensive approach to planning and service delivery had been hindered by the absence of 100 per cent funding for some services, such as diversion.

Throughcare was considered by Main Consultation Group interviewees and managers to be an area that was still under developed, despite local authority plans identifying this as an area of priority. Reasons for the slow progress in developing throughcare provided by managers and some Main Consultation Group interviewees included: the relative priority which prison management attributed to the service; the separate funding of social work in prisons; it is resource intensive on account of travel costs and staff time; and the relatively low number of offenders receiving throughcare services.

ORGANISATIONAL STRUCTURES

The shift to greater specialisation and the introduction of the National Standards were viewed by managers, court social workers and some sheriffs, as having resulted in improvements in the preparation of Social Enquiry Reports (SERs) and probation. However, McIvor and Barry (1998) found that the National Standards were most closely met in the area whose teams were less specialised. On the other hand, managers considered that the areas in which the greatest progress had been made in introducing more structured offence focused methods of probation work, were those which had the clearest specialist structures.

MONITORING

Whilst in most authorities significant progress had been made in monitoring the quality of services, less emphasis had been placed upon the development of methods to evaluate services, in particular one-to-one work with offenders. Systems for monitoring and evaluating the effectiveness of prison based social work services were thought by Main Consultation Group interviewees and managers to be less well developed.

Interviewees acknowledged that the delay in fully implementing the National Core Data System (NCDS) had hindered local planning and a national review of policy implementation. However, steps had been taken to review the system. Main Consultation Group respondents identified a need for the development of a strategic overview of policy and priorities but acknowledged that the Group did not meet sufficiently frequently to undertake a rigorous review of policy implementation at a national level.

CONCLUSION

The research was conducted in the early stages of policy implementation and some aspects of implementation were not complete. Certain aspects of implementation at the national level facilitated local policy implementation:

- Involvement of key stakeholders in preparing the National Standards.
- The national planning process enhanced local strategic planning.

Other aspects of national implementation hindered local implementation:

- The absence of 100 per cent funding for all services hindered the development of a comprehensive approach to planning and service delivery.
- Sufficient funding was not made available to provide the full range and level of specialist services identified in local plans.
- Early planning procedures were not found to be totally effective.
- Delays in implementing the NCDS and providing feedback of national statistics and inspections hindered national and local reviews of policy implementation.
- The separate funding and priority allocated to social work in prisons was seen by some interviewees to be partly attributable to the slow progress in developing throughcare services.

CHAPTER ONE

BACKGROUND TO THE STUDY

INTRODUCTION

In Scotland, statutory social work services to offenders and their families are provided by the local authority social work departments. Since April 1991, the Scottish Office has reimbursed to social work departments the full costs of providing a range of statutory social work services in the criminal justice system. National Objectives and Standards (the National Standards) were introduced by the Social Work Services Group of the Scottish Office to coincide with the introduction of the funding initiative. The aim of the National Standards is to promote the development of high quality management and practice, the most efficient and effective use of resources and to provide social work services to the criminal justice system which have the confidence of both the courts and the wider public.

The National Standards and the funding initiative cover: social enquiry reports; court social work services; probation; community service[1]; and throughcare (social work in prisons is funded by the Scottish Prison Service). Since 1991, the initiative has been extended to supervised release orders, bail information and accommodation schemes, and supervised attendance order schemes (the latter two schemes are not yet available on a national basis). It is intended to include diversion from prosecution in the 100 per cent funding arrangement, subject to the progress of pilot schemes established in 1996. At present, fine supervision, means enquiry reports and deferred sentence supervision are not included in the funding initiative.

Prior to the introduction of the 100 per cent funding initiative and the National Standards, local authorities had to fund the majority of social work services out of their general income. Criminal justice services were, therefore, in competition for resources with other local authority services and as a result were not always of sufficient quantity and quality to meet the requirements of the courts.

The main aims of the Government's policy are[2]:

- to reduce the use of custody by increasing the availability, improving the quality and targeting the use of community based court disposals and throughcare services on those most at risk of custody, especially young adult repeat offenders;
- to enable offenders to address their offending behaviour and make a successful adjustment to law abiding life.

BACKGROUND TO THE RESEARCH

Central Government's review and evaluation of implementation of the funding initiative and the National Standards involves a programme of inspection by Social Work Services Inspectorate (SWSI), interpretation of statistics and a programme of research.

The research programme is being conducted in three phases. The main purpose of Phase One, which was undertaken in 1992-1993, was to examine the responses of key criminal justice decision makers and Scottish Office officials to the principal objectives of the policy and the early arrangements for its implementation (McAra, 1998). Phase Two (of which this study is a part) consists of five inter-related studies, conducted in 1994-1995, which examine progress towards policy objectives: the national and local context of policy implementation (Brown, Levy and McIvor, 1998); sentencer decision-making (Brown and Levy, 1998); Parole Board decision-making (McAra, 1998a); the process and outcomes of probation (McIvor and Barry, 1998); and the process and outcomes of throughcare (McIvor and Barry, 1998a). Phase Three will look at the longer term impact of services for offenders.

Four sheriff court areas, each in separate social work authorities, were selected as study sites for the research programme to reflect areas of both high and low population density and to represent both specialist and more generic forms of organising social work criminal justice services. The names of the four areas have been anonymised in reports and are referred to as Scott, Wallace, Burns and Bruce.

The purpose of this study is to describe the national and local context within which the policy was developed, implemented and reviewed prior to and during the period in which the research programme was conducted.

---

[1] The 100 per cent funding initiative and National Objectives and Standards were first applied to community service in 1989.

[2] Evaluation Strategy Working Group, September 1990. More recent statements (the 1996 White Paper on Crime and Punishment, paragraphs 9.1 and 10.3) are consistent with these aims.

The study examines the implementation of the policy at the national level and the way in which the policy was implemented at the local level. The study identifies those factors which have facilitated or inhibited policy implementation and which therefore impact on progress towards policy objectives.

There are three main stages in the process of introducing a new policy: development of objectives, priorities, targets and standards of service delivery; implementation; and review of implementation. Success of this process depends on the effectiveness of the mechanisms of: consultation and collaboration; planning and funding; service provision; and monitoring and evaluation. Chapter Two describes the effectiveness of procedures for consultation and planning. Chapter Three examines the impact of consultation and planning on service provision in respect of different organisational structures and local arrangements. Chapter Four describes the process of review of policy implementation with a focus on monitoring and evaluation. Finally, Chapter Five describes the key issues and conclusions.

Methods

This joint study was undertaken in 1995 by The Scottish Office Central Research Unit (CRU) and the Social Work Research Centre (SWRC) at Stirling University. Findings are based on an analysis of central and local government policy and planning documents; semi-structured interviews with five members of the Main Consultation Group on Social Work Services to the Criminal Justice System selected to represent the range of stakeholders from the Group; semi-structured interviews with 12 middle and senior social work managers in the four study authorities with responsibility for criminal justice services; and semi-structured interviews with seven independent sector service providers operating in the study areas. Reference is made in the report to the findings of other studies in the research programme, where appropriate.

The Context of the Study

The National Standards describe the responsibilities of central and local government. These are summarised below to provide the context in which policy implementation, review and development take place.

The Secretary of State, advised by the Social Work Services Group (SWSG) of the Scottish Office Home Department, is responsible for setting national objectives, priorities, targets and standards for the delivery of social work services in the criminal justice system. Social Work Services Group is responsible for promulgating national objectives and standards and issuing administrative and professional guidance as required to achieve their efficient and effective implementation. Social Work Services Group is required to consider the range and level of resources required to meet the objectives and standards of those services eligible for 100 per cent funding, in consultation with local authorities, the independent sector and other interested parties, and to provide funds accordingly. Social Work Services Inspectorate in close co-operation with Social Work Services Group is also responsible for inspecting[3] and reviewing the extent to which the policy is being efficiently and effectively implemented and to establish a National Core Data System (NCDS) in consultation with interested parties to monitor and evaluate policy implementation. Social Work Services Group is required to consult with social work and with criminal justice agencies so that they may contribute to the formulation and review of Central Government policies for social work in the criminal justice system.

Local authorities are responsible for the efficient and effective organisation, management, delivery and purchase of services within the framework set out by the Standards. In consultation with the judiciary, the independent sector and other agencies, they are responsible for preparing and revising strategic plans in accordance with the National Standards. Local authorities are responsible for devising information systems in consultation with other interested parties to assist planning and delivery of services, and the regular monitoring and evaluation of performance and outcomes, and to provide Central Government with the information it requires. Prison social workers are employed by the local authorities but their services are funded by the Scottish Prison Service (SPS) which achieved separate agency status in April 1993 and is funded by The Scottish Office.

The key stakeholders in criminal justice social work policy are Central Government, local authorities, the judiciary, the police, the parole board, the prison service, those independent sector agencies with an interest in providing services, and health services. Other agencies with an interest in developing or providing criminal justice services include housing and those working in community care.

---

[3] Inspections are carried out on behalf of SWSG by the Social Work Services Inspectorate (SWSI).

CHAPTER TWO
CONSULTATION AND PLANNING

INTRODUCTION

Successful implementation of the policy depends, to a great extent, on the effectiveness of consultation and planning. National and local consultation is required to harness the skills and experience of a wide range of stakeholders, to achieve a sense of ownership of the National Standards, and to ensure that sentencers and criminal justice agencies have confidence in the credibility and effectiveness of services. Effective planning is required to set the objectives, priorities and targets at the national and local levels and effective allocation of funding is required to ensure that these can be achieved. The purpose of this chapter is to describe the level and assess the effectiveness of consultation and planning at both the national and local levels.

CONSULTATION

National Consultation

The Main Consultation Group (the Group) was established to facilitate national consultation and communication. The effectiveness of national consultation, as reflected in the operation of the Main Consultation Group, can be assessed by examining the extent to which key stakeholders were involved in developing the National Standards; tensions within the Group were managed; members had a clear understanding of the roles of other members; and members represented the views of their organisations.

Involvement of Key Stakeholders

The Main Consultation Group was established in 1989 with the specific remit to review social work criminal justice services and to oversee production of the initial National Objectives and Standards. Key stakeholders were actively involved in the development of the National Standards either by being members of the Main Consultation Group, being co-opted onto one of the subgroups developing a particular section of the Standards, or receiving draft Standards for comment. The membership of the Main Consultation Group at the time of the development of the National Standards included: Central Government; local authorities; the judiciary; the police; professional social work; and the voluntary sector. Membership now includes the Scottish Prisons Service. Membership of the subgroups included representatives of the organisations represented on the Main Consultation Group and the universities.

The effectiveness of the Group was generally considered by Main Consultation Group interviewees to have been diminished by the infrequency of meetings (it meets on an annual basis). This was seen to inhibit the development of working relationships amongst members which had existed when the Standards were being developed. On the other hand, Main Consultation Group respondents considered that the Group had been most successful in involving key stakeholders in developing, and generating a sense of corporate ownership of, the National Standards.

Managing Tensions

At interview, Main Consultation Group interviewees considered that the Group had been most effective in providing a forum in which differing views could be expressed and explored, although differences were not always resolved. Meetings were described by non-government interviewees as being driven by the Scottish Office rather than allowing members to identify their priorities and issues. The Scottish Office's role was described in interview as being to achieve consensus about policy development. However, some non-government interviewees noted that there was no mechanism to resolve dispute if potentially contentious areas were raised:

> "Sometimes the response is to block if there is a problem, so (that) it's not an issue for this setting but ... would be looked at elsewhere. The honest response is avoiding any risk of confrontation in the group." (MCG5)[4]

[4] Main Consultation Group interview five.

Despite this, however, most Main Consultation Group respondents considered that the Group had facilitated a better understanding of the interests, constraints and viewpoints of other members, rather than:

> "A continued grumbling about social work and criminal justice, without it being focused." (MCG5)

Roles of Members of the Group and Level of Representation

The role of The Scottish Office was generally regarded as being to service and facilitate meetings. Scottish Office representatives saw their role as identifying any shifts in direction or emphasis which might detract from the most efficient or effective pursuit of improving the quality of services.

Respondents saw the role of the local authority representatives as being to inform the Group of the practical implications of managing and delivering policy intentions and services. In addition, local authority membership facilitated the support and pursuit of the policy and enabled authorities to be supported by action at the centre. Their role was also seen to be to ensure that:

> "...issues just didn't get lost and the one of mentally disturbed offenders is still not being tackled at all. It's a key problem in the prisons sector. The linkages, I think, with the prison service is a weakness." (MCG5)

Local authorities had mechanisms for obtaining views both from within their local area and across Scotland, through the Association of Directors of Social Work (ADSW). The Main Consultation Group was a forum for voicing these views.

Main Consultation Group respondents recognised that the independent sector had a role in considering whether the Standards were workable. By offering the viewpoint of prospective service providers, they could advise on objectives and strategies for policy development to enable more coherent and responsive services to be given to users. It was acknowledged that it was difficult for the single independent sector member on the Main Consultation Group to represent the sector as a whole.

Interviewees considered that judicial representation on the Group provided sentencers' with an experience of the operation of the policy and advice on court perspectives on putting policy into practice, and could ensure that the Standards and services had the support and confidence of the judiciary in Scotland. It was, however, suggested in interview that judicial representatives should be restricted to those who had extensive experience of community based disposals and were informed of the issues. Although some respondents considered that the judiciary were extremely conscientious about sounding out their colleagues before meetings, others thought that they tended to express personal views and did not have a mechanism for collecting views across Scotland. One interviewee suggested that:

> "One might have looked to the judiciary for more assistance in developing the contribution which government could have made to the evolution of judicial attitudes, consciousness raising amongst the judiciary of what is going on, and ... the pursuit of a more consistent and coherent judicial response to the development of these services. Maybe through training, for example, participation in developing the judicial side of it and enabling inputs into judicial training around this area of service." (MCG2)

Whilst the Main Consultation Group was the principal mechanism for national consultation with the judiciary, other forms of consultation took place, for example, a conference at which SWSG explained the 100 per cent funding initiative and new arrangements. A judicial member of the Main Consultation Group explained in interview that this took place in the early stages of policy implementation and appeared to be successful as sheriffs viewed it as a helpful forum in which they could examine and discuss the policy and the way in which it affected them. It was suggested that this forum had been successful in increasing sentencers' understanding of and confidence in social work services provided under the new initiative. As a result of the new arrangements, a judicial interviewee considered that the level of confidence in social work services had improved:

> "One doesn't have to go very far back before you found flare-ups or sounding off about deficiencies, that were either real or perceived, in social work services - these became quite embarrassing and were rather public at times." (MCG1)

Local Consultation/Liaison

Main Consultation Group interviewees provided views about consultation and liaison at the local level. In most instances, these coincided with views of social work managers. For example, the National Standards were considered to have reinforced the need for liaison and to have facilitated the development of connections between local authorities and other key stakeholders. This was seen to be necessary to create the consensus within which local services could operate.

The Judiciary

Some representatives of the Main Consultation Group and sheriffs interviewed in the sentencer decision making study (Brown and Levy, 1998) stressed the importance of establishing relationships with people, especially court liaison officers, and being able to relate to and have confidence in them. They considered that there was a general feeling that sheriffs could be approached more readily than before and that sheriffs now knew what standards social work services should meet.

Although social work managers did not consider that liaison arrangements had changed significantly as a result of the policy, in all areas they reported that liaison with the judiciary had improved at the local level. Managers said that local authorities usually consulted the judiciary on proposed developments, changes in resources, disposals and services and this was seen to be helpful in determining what services should be available and to ensure that the services were used. Liaison meetings also provided sentencers with an opportunity to offer feedback to local authorities regarding the effectiveness of services provided to the courts.

The liaison arrangements in the four study areas are shown in Table 1.1:

Table 1.1: Liaison Arrangements with Courts

	Formal	Informal
Scott	Court social worker attends the bi-monthly Court Consultative Committee.	Ad hoc liaison between court social workers and sheriffs, and between social workers and procurators fiscal.
Wallace	Sheriffs attend annual formal liaison meetings with senior social work managers.	Ad hoc liaison between court social workers and sheriffs and between social workers and procurators fiscal.
Burns	Sheriffs attend annual formal liaison meetings with senior social work managers. Team managers attend quarterly court users' meetings.	Ad hoc liaison between court social workers and sheriffs and between social workers and procurators fiscal.
Bruce	Sheriff attends local team's annual review meeting.	Ad hoc liaison between sheriffs and court social workers and district manager. Ad hoc liaison between social workers and procurators fiscal

In only two of the four study courts (Wallace and Burns) did sheriffs attend formal liaison meetings with senior social work managers. The function of formal liaison meetings (in areas where these took place) and their effectiveness, were seen by social work managers and sheriffs (Brown and Levy, 1998)[5] to vary across authorities: where specific issues were discussed, they were viewed as useful, but where the focus was on more general policy issues, they were seen to be less effective. The 1992 SWSI inspection on the progress towards policy implementation[6] suggested that links between local authorities and the judiciary would be improved if the purpose of meetings were clarified. Social work managers and court social workers (Brown and Levy, 1998) reported that social work items were not always included on the agenda of the Court Consultative Committee meetings in Scott and the court users' meetings in Burns. However, informal liaison, in particular between sheriffs and court social workers, was seen by social work managers and sheriffs (Brown and Levy, 1998) as being more effective. The opportunity to communicate effectively with all sentencers was lessened in courts which used a high number of visiting sheriffs.

Although relationships between sentencers and social work staff were generally described in positive terms, gaps were identified in two authorities which, if filled, might have improved the effectiveness of liaison. Senior managers in Scott were reported historically to have had a poor relationship with local sentencers as a consequence of which there were no formal mechanisms for liaison at this level. Likewise in Bruce there was

5 The views of sheriffs in the four study areas were obtained in the sentencer decision-making study (Brown and Levy, 1998).

6 SWSI (1993) *Social Work Services in the Criminal Justice System: Achieving National Standards -Progress Report*. Social Work Services Inspectorate for Scotland. Members of the inspection team visited each authority. Authorities and voluntary organisations were also asked to complete a questionnaire.

said to be little opportunity, other than through the annual review meeting at which the specialist team's performance was discussed, for the practice team manager to liaise with the sheriff on a regular basis (however, the sheriff did liaise regularly with the district manager).

The findings of the inspection (SWSI, 1993) and interviews with sheriffs (Brown and Levy, 1998) reported that some sheriffs had declined invitations to attend liaison meetings. The inspection concluded that:

> "Readiness on the part of all judges to participate in liaison would assist service development and there may be scope for further action by The Scottish Office to encourage local dialogue."
>
> (SWSI, 1993, p.16)

Some sheriffs interviewed in the sentencer decision making study indicated that they would welcome more details on the success of probation and commmunity service orders than that provided in termination reports, especially for "high risk" offenders. However, formal liaison meetings should provide a forum for feedback on how offenders performed and the success in orders and it is evident that, in some areas, the sheriffs' need for this information was not being met.

Liaison with Procurators Fiscal

Some Main Consultation Group members considered that the proposed inclusion of diversion within 100 per cent funding had given impetus to the development of links with procurators fiscal and to the development of more coherent systems for interacting with court agencies.

Interviews with social work managers indicated that, although more formal and structured arrangements had been introduced in two areas, liaison with procurators fiscal was generally conducted on an informal basis at a local level and tended to focus upon particular initiatives such as bail services or diversion. Managers pointed to the difficulty of establishing a regular forum for liaison with procurators fiscal whose workloads precluded the development of more structured arrangements but they and those procurators fiscal who were interviewed, generally considered that existing arrangements were satisfactory.

Liaison with Central Government

Social work managers commented on the importance of effective links with The Scottish Office which had been facilitated by the identification of key personnel within authorities who were responsible for liaison with Central Government. Other factors which, where they were present, were said by managers to have facilitated policy implementation, included good support from senior management and effective communication within departments, including links with other areas of social work.

The Independent Sector

Liaison between local authorities and the independent sector was one area in which the views of Main Consultation Group interviewees did not coincide with the views of social work managers and independent sector providers. It was suggested by Main Consultation Group respondents that networks between local authorities and the independent sector could have been exploited to a greater extent. It was noted by representatives of the Main Consultation Group that in only a few regions had there been an opportunity for the independent sector to consult with the social work department and other interests at a regional level. It was suggested that the agenda at these meetings was driven by the social work department and that other interest groups had to adopt a passive role, commenting on statistics and the strategic plan rather than taking a more active role.

Contrary to the views expressed by the Main Consultation Group interviewees, independent sector providers and social work managers believed that an appropriate level of consultation had been undertaken in the context of the local authority strategic planning process and considered that, in general, the nature and extent of liaison with the local authority in relation to both policy and operational matters had been adequate. This was confirmed by the inspection (SWSI, 1993). Mechanisms for liaising with the independent sector varied across authorities and were, in general, determined by the funding relationship with the local authority and the level of direct co-operation required to provide the service. In the case of Urban Aided projects, local authority managers met regularly with project managers to review progress and discuss strategic and practical issues.

Independent sector providers identified a number of factors that they believed had facilitated the development of effective working relationships with the local authority: a sense of shared ownership or shared recognition of the need for a particular service; the creation of clear lines of communication (the existence of a named individual in the local authority with whom independent sector providers could liaise); and clarity regarding the local authority's expectations and the formal systems which had been put in place to establish and maintain accountability on the part of the independent sector.

Independent sector providers also identified factors which had possibly prevented their relationship in some local authorities from being more productive: the absence of service agreements; the lack of regular contact with social work teams to ensure a consistent flow of referrals; staff turnover in the local authority resulting in less familiarisation with the operation of projects; being less willing to engage in work on a partnership basis; and the lack of a forum for joint discussion of strategic issues with other organisations in the independent sector and with the local authority.

The independent sector service providers who were interviewed clearly saw themselves as involved in a partnership arrangement with local authorities, providing a range of services which complemented those being delivered directly by the statutory sector. The strongest sense of partnership was said to be felt when the local authority and the independent sector provider were involved jointly in managing and delivering different aspects of a service. Since the introduction of 100 per cent funding and the National Standards, relationships between the local authority and the independent sector were perceived as having become more formal (mainly through service agreements) and it was suggested that there was now a greater degree of accountability on the part of the independent sector.

Liaison between The Scottish Prison Service and Social Work Criminal Justice Services

Representatives of the Main Consultation Group indicated that liaison between the Scottish Prison Service (SPS) and social work criminal justice services could be more effective. The 1992 SWSI inspection of social work units in prisons[7] found that little or no consultation with social work management had taken place when SPS introduced its Sentence Planning Initiative. This was despite good relationships between prison and social work managers and the existence of formal structures to ensure co-ordination of effort. However, the inspection found that in four units there was no system for formal meetings between the governor grade with a responsibility for social work and the head of the social work unit, as required in *Continuity Through Co-operation.*[8] SPS had, however, convened an interagency group including an independent agency to consider relationships with prisons. It was considered that links between SPS and SWSG were improving, but that the Parole Board should also be involved in liaison.

At the local level, formal arrangements for liaison between local authority social work departments and prisons located within their geographical boundaries were believed by most managers to be reasonably satisfactory. Managers reported that the primary focus for liaison with the prison service was the production and review of social work unit management plans. However, communication between field social workers and those in prisons were not seen by some Main Consultation Group respondents to be effective.

Interviews with managers revealed that few formal mechanisms for cross-authority liaison had been established and liaison tended to take place on a case-by-case basis. The absence of formal arrangements was attributed by managers to logistical difficulties which would arguably be compounded by the creation of a larger number of smaller authorities following local government reform.

PLANNING

The Planning Process

Prior to the introduction of the National Standards, local authorities varied in their approach towards, and ability to undertake, effective strategic planning. Submission of formal strategic plans to SWSG was first introduced with the implementation of the National Standards in 1991. The purpose of these plans is to ensure that the resources and the skills available within local authorities and elsewhere in the community are used to best effect in meeting the National Standards[9]. They are also intended to assist managers and practitioners by providing direction to service development and as a means of measuring performance and outcomes. Annual National Planning Statements are prepared by SWSG in consultation with COSLA[10] and

---

[7] *National Inspection of Prison-Based Social Work Units.* Social Work Inspectorate for Scotland, 1993. The inspection was undertaken in seven prison based social work units, where Inspectors interviewed social work and prison staff, managers and prisoners. The seven units were representative of the range of prisons throughout Scotland.

[8] SPS/SWSG (1989). *Continuity Through Co-operation: A National Framework of Policy and Practice Guidance for Social Work in Scottish Penal Establishments.*

[9] The National Standards planning principles are listed in Annex II.

[10] Convention of Scottish Local Authorities.

other criminal justice interests, and are intended to assist and inform authorities on the resources and other planning assumptions that should underpin preparation of the local plans.

Review of the Planning Process

The findings of the inspection suggested that the review should take into account:

- The need for strategic plans to be drawn up with clear assumptions about the likely level of resources available;
- The need for some flexibility in the way resources are allocated to take account of fluctuations in demand;
- The need for efficiency savings as a means of releasing resources to improve and develop the service;
- The need for a simplified common planning framework.

(SWSI, 1993, p.14).

Following the inspection of progress towards policy implementation (SWSI, 1993) a joint COSLA/SWSG Strategic Planning Review Group was established in 1993 as it was evident that the planning system was not operating effectively. At the first meeting of the Review Group[11] SWSG stated that it sought to disentangle the national strategic planning requirement from local operational planning, resulting in plans being prepared on a more commonly based structure with clear priorities and resource assumptions being conveyed by Central Government. It was intended that this would result in a planning system that could be operated in less time and would allow the plan to be more realistic.

The main changes in the planning procedure instigated by the Strategic Planning Review Group were that the information required by SWSG would be provided annually based on a standardised format, but local authorities would prepare a full strategic planning statement every three years and update these in years one and two. Under the revised planning arrangements, local authorities were required: to review performance against the previous year's service objectives and targets in a standardised format; to identify detailed objectives and estimated service outcomes during the following financial year; and to identify broad service objectives in each of the subsequent two years[12]. Pilot planning standards were developed and guidance based on the pilot was to be issued to new authorities by March 1996.

The review was considered by managers to have been helpful in identifying redundant information as the previous exercise was considered to have been "more ambitious than could be digested". Managers, however, suggested that SWSG should improve the speed with which it analyses the plans and gives responses to local authorities.

Effectiveness of Planning

The planning process was seen by some Main Consultation Group respondents and managers to impose an intellectual discipline on business, in that it focused on: what was to be achieved within available resources; priorities; evidence of need; and assessment of performance. It was seen by some Main Consultation Group respondents to have disciplined the local authorities to conduct internal reviews which were consistent throughout Scotland and involved a range of interest groups (although others suggested that this may have been more "rhetoric than reality"). However, Main Consultation Group interviews suggested that the focus of the plans ought to be widened beyond the criminal justice arena to take account of other services, such as health and housing.

The planning process was believed by some managers to have engendered a greater sense of ownership of the policy and service objectives amongst practitioners. Some managers indicated that a significant feature of the planning process was the need to anticipate the likely resource implications of new policies and legislation to ensure that the service was adequately resourced to meet new demands. The Criminal Justice Bill and the Prisoners and Criminal Proceedings (Scotland) Act 1993 were cited by managers as the main examples of legislative developments which impacted upon social work criminal justice services. The main difficulty encountered in anticipating the impact of, for example, changes in the provisions for supervised attendance orders or the introduction of supervised release orders and non-parole licences, was said by managers to be that they necessarily had limited information upon which to make planning assumptions.

---

[11] Minutes of the COSLA/SWSG Strategic Planning Review Group, November 1993.

[12] The planning system was reviewed and new National Standards and procedures introduced in 1994 to reflect planning experience to date. Further guidance was issued in April 1995 on the interim arrangements for planning subsequent to local government reorganisation.

Content of Plans

A feature of the early plans of the four study authorities was their focus upon achieving National Standards in the core areas of service delivery. However, the plans in each area reported that a lack of information had hampered an assessment of the degree of compliance with the Standards. Subsequent plans placed greater emphasis upon consolidating progress made in the core areas of service delivery rather than expanding services, and more recent plans reflected a greater emphasis upon service development. In plans a high priority was accorded to providing services to young offenders and remittal to the Children's Hearings System. In each authority, services to persistent young adult offenders at risk of custody were being provided mainly through intensive probation programmes. However, in the study of early arrangements (McAra, 1998), concerns were expressed that insufficient attention had been given to the development of schemes aimed at young people involved in less serious offences, and this view was supported by the analysis of local authority plans. Plans identified the need for expansion of existing services and the introduction of new initiatives but social work managers and later plans stated that funding for most of these proposals was not available within the authority or additional funding was not provided by the Scottish Office to enable these proposals to be implemented.

Some sheriffs identified a need for additional specialist services in their area and that this could influence their use of a community based disposal in some cases (Brown and Levy, 1998). Respondents in the study of early arrangements (McAra, 1998) believed throughcare to be the least well developed service prior to policy implementation and therefore had the most progress to make. In the present study it was found that each of the four study areas had identified community based throughcare as a key target for further development in their plans from 1993. Social work managers acknowledged that throughcare was the area in which least progress had been made. There was a variety of explanations offered by managers for the relative lack of progress in this area of work: it was resource intensive in terms of travel costs and staff time and it dealt with a lower volume of offenders than other services.

In addition the misalignment of local authority and prison plans was said by managers to have detracted from the quality of prison social work services: the different time-scales for the preparation of local authority strategic plans for social work criminal justice services and prison management plans, and the format for local authority plans, did not fit with the planning format adopted by the Scottish Prison Service. Disappointment was expressed by some managers that prison social work had only been included in local authority plans in the most recent planning cycle.

Allocation of Funding

Central Government finance was recognised by social work managers as being crucial to the planning process. The later National Planning Statements, in identifying Central Government priorities and indicating the financial assumptions upon which local plans should be based, had, some social work managers suggested, made the planning process more realistic:

> "In the early planning documents we were planning out the direction of where we thought the service should go and asking for money - basically bidding for money to do that. But in fact these plans turned out to be completely useless because the money we got bore no relation to our plans. In a sense the planning - all the effort that went into it - was a waste of time...I think we in one way welcomed the new approach because it is more realistic...When we get told before we start our planning what the parameters are, what we'll get new money for, what we won't get new money for, at least our output is now more focused upon what might be achievable." (Social work manager).

Other managers, however, believed that there was still an element of uncertainty when plans were prepared about the extent to which the proposals contained in them would be funded. A representative of the Consultation Group said that there had been an unsuccessful attempt to establish a formula and that the allocation of funding was essentially idiosyncratic :

> "There is no formula and there is no justice in the system as far as I see. Special pleading is more likely to be more effective than national debate." (MCG5)

The inspection (SWSI, 1993) identified variations in workloads of staff within and between regions and suggested that there may be some scope for greater cost efficiency. However, in the present study concerns were expressed by social work management about funding being too closely tied to workload measures. A decrease in the number of probation orders, it was argued, did not necessarily equate with a decrease in the resources required to supervise probationers since orders were now being made at a higher point in the sentencing tariff. Managers were concerned that the current funding arrangements failed to recognise the resource implications of undertaking effective work with high tariff offenders. The attendant risk was that National Standards might be met without associated increases in the quality and effectiveness of practice.

The Scottish Office interviewees were asked about the allocation of funding. It was explained that funding for individual authorities was now based on trends in demand, the amount of money available, priorities for new service activity and the undertaking, given to COSLA, that existing local authorities would not receive less than they did before 100 per cent funding was introduced. The capacity to reallocate resources to develop services currently under developed (for example, throughcare) had therefore been constrained more than Central Government would have wanted. Although in recent years the available funding had increased in real terms, this had been spent on service innovation rather than in altering the balance amongst authorities.

A range of methods was used by authorities to make the most efficient and effective use of limited resources. Examples provided by managers included achieving efficiency gains in an area of service delivery to enable other services to be provided for which Central Government funding had not been secured. Authorities would, in addition, submit occasional bids for extra funding, either through the strategic planning process or on an 'opportunistic' basis. In general, however, managers highlighted the need to prioritise carefully to ensure that standards in the core areas of service delivery were met. This might be at the cost of introducing more innovative, and potentially more effective, methods of work:

> "A number of probation group work initiatives started by social workers in specialist teams have not survived because we would have needed more staffing resources to maintain them...If you ask most teams why they don't do some things that they have tried and don't maintain, it is because they're too busy trying to meet core service requirements of National Standards - SERs and supervising probation orders - without actually doing the more sophisticated bits of work."
>
> (Social Work Manager)

CONCLUSION

The National Standards emphasise the importance of developing good liaison arrangements with sentencers and the independent sector to ensure that the new arrangements operate well (SWSG 1991, part 1, paragraph 107). At the national level, consultation was seen to be successful in involving key stakeholders in developing, and generating a sense of ownership of, the National Standards. At the local level, informal liaison with the judiciary and liaison with the independent sector were generally considered to operate effectively. However, formal liaison between sheriffs and senior social work managers and between prisons and social work departments in another authority could, it was believed, be improved in some areas.

It was found that the initial planning procedures, introduced on a national level, did not operate effectively at the local level and that the absence of reliable national and local information systems hindered local planning. Steps have been taken to remedy these problems: revised planning procedures have been introduced and the system for providing national information on policy implementation has been reviewed (Chapter Four).

Nevertheless, there were still some concerns about obtaining funding for developing existing services, establishing additional specialist services and introducing more innovative methods of work. The absence of appropriate specialist services could, some sheriffs argued, dissuade them from imposing a non-custodial sentence in some cases. If the courts' needs for services are not met, this could inhibit the achievement of policy objectives.

CHAPTER THREE
SERVICE PROVISION

INTRODUCTION

This chapter examines the outcome of consultation and planning by exploring the impact of different organisational structures and characteristics of each of the four study areas on service delivery. Firstly, the characteristics of the study areas are described to illustrate the differences between them. An assessment is then made of the impact on service delivery arrangements of differing organisational structures and demographic features, and the planning and funding procedures.

CHARACTERISTICS OF THE STUDY AREAS

A summary of the characteristics of each area is provided in Table 3.1, including: organisational structures; the characteristics of the samples from two of the studies in the research programme (the probationers in McIvor and Barry, 1998, and those receiving throughcare, McIvor and Barry, 1998a); and the specialist services which were available in each of the four study sites at the time of the research. The dates refer to the year in which the service was established. It should be noted that where a specialist service did not exist, social workers often provided support on an individual basis.

The study sites were selected to reflect areas of both high and low population density and to represent both specialist and more generic forms of organising social work criminal justice services. In addition, table 3.1 shows that the areas also differed in respect of their sentencing trends, offender gravity and the level and type of provisions of specialist services.

The courts in Burns and Bruce, both of which cover a rural area, had below the national average use of custody compared to Scott and Wallace, which are situated in more densely populated areas and had above the national average use of custody. The offenders in the Bruce sample tended to be of a much lower 'tariff' (in respect of previous convictions, custodial sentences and risk of custody) than those in Scott and Wallace. Bruce and Scott, which had a more generic organisational structure than the other areas, had fewer specialist services for offenders than Burns and Wallace.

Table 3.1: Characteristics of the Study Areas

	Scott	Wallace	Burns	Bruce
Area Type	Large town bordering urban area.	City.	Large town in rural area.	Small town in rural area.
Social Work Organisation	Up to 80 per cent of social workers' time allocated to CJ work. Generic middle management. Specialisation in 1991.	Specialist up to senior management level. Specialisation in 1990.	Specialist up to middle management level. Specialisation in 1991.	Specialist with generic middle management level. Specialisation in 1992.
Court Features	Large court. Above national average use of custody, CS & PO. Below average use of fines.	Large court. Above national average use of custody, CS & PO. Below average use of fines.	Medium court. Below national average use of custody. About average use of CS, PO & fines.	Small court. Below national average use of custody and fines. Above average use of CS & PO
Study Samples				
Offender Gravity:	Medium-High*	High*	+	Low*
PO breached:	Medium (19%)	High (39%)	+	Low (4%)
Specialist Services				
Intensive Probation:	SWD (1988)	Independent (1991)	Independent (1991)	None
Substance Misuse:	SWD (1991)	Independent (pre-1991)	SWD (1995)	Independent (1992)
Alcohol Misuse:	Independent (1990)	Independent (pre-1991)	Independent (1991)	Independent (1990)
Mental Health:	Independent (1992)	SWD (1993)	None	None
Sex Offenders:	None	SWD (1990)	None	None
Domestic Violence:	None	None	Independent (1991)	None
Employment:	None	Independent (1990)	Independent (1991)	Independent (1992)
Supported Accommodation:	None	Independent (1990-94)	Independent (1992)	None

+ There were insufficient numbers in the probation and throughcare study samples in this area on which to base an assessment.

* This assessment was based on the number of previous convictions, the number of previous custodial sentences and assessments of risk of custody made by the author of the SER. A full description of the samples are provided in the individual study reports.

Organisational Structures of the Study Sites

In Scott, services were delivered at district level by practitioners in split posts, each of whom devoted a percentage of their time to offender services and the remainder to generic social work tasks. They were managed by senior social workers who likewise were employed in criminal justice/generic split posts. They, in turn, were accountable to generic area team managers and district managers. Planning and co-ordination functions were performed by a district co-ordinator who had no line management responsibilities in respect of area team staff but provided line management for other criminal justice services delivered by staff located outwith the area teams. At the regional level centralised strategic planning and co-ordination functions were undertaken by specialist managers.

In Bruce, criminal justice social work services were delivered by teams of specialist practitioners led by a specialist practice team manager. The practice team managers were accountable, in turn, to generic district managers. Operational management and strategic planning and co-ordination functions had been separated. The lead officer for offender services was located in the planning and co-ordination branch of the department.

In Burns, social work services to the criminal justice system were delivered by three teams of specialist social workers each of which was led by a specialist team manager. An overview of service planning, development and delivery was provided by a regional manager for criminal justice services. Offender services were located within the adult assessment section of the department which includes community care.

The greatest degree of specialisation could be found in Wallace which had introduced specialist arrangements for service delivery and management to the level of assistant director. In this authority social work services to offenders were delivered by specialist social workers located in teams in each of the three districts.

IMPACT OF AREA CHARACTERISTICS ON SERVICE DELIVERY

It was found that there were three characteristics which impacted on service delivery: whether the area was mainly urban or rural; the size of the court; and the level of specialisation of the organisational structures.

Rural Areas

Rural areas were said by managers and social workers (Brown and Levy, 1998) to have experienced particular difficulties in accessing or providing specialist services. The relatively low numbers of offenders referred precluded the development of locally based initiatives, and served as a disincentive to organisations providing services in more densely populated areas to extend their services on an outreach basis to outlying areas. However, in one rural area (Bruce), an independent sector provider operated an employment service for offenders on an outreach basis. Even if services were available in neighbouring urban areas, managers and social workers (Brown and Levy, 1998) indicated that offenders in rural areas were often reluctant, for practical or territorial reasons, to make use of services outwith their local environment. This was especially evident in relation to accessing supported accommodation, which was unevenly distributed and tended to be concentrated in the cities. Managers identified difficulties in meeting time-scales for contacts with probationers in rural areas as a result of distances to be travelled and arranging convenient appointments with probationers.

In rural areas, difficulties were sometimes encountered in providing an appropriate intensive probation course due to the low level of demand at any one time. One sheriff indicated that this might discourage him from imposing a probation order (Brown and Levy, 1998).

Managers believed that the relatively low numbers of offenders receiving throughcare meant that there was a gap in management and staff expertise, particularly in rural areas where there was less opportunity to obtain experience and develop skills in this area of work. Even in more densely populated areas the costs of providing an effective throughcare service consistent with National Standards were, managers believed, significantly increased if it required making contact with individual prisoners in institutions located at some distance from their home area.

Size of Court

Larger courts tended to use a high number of temporary sheriffs but liaison with temporary sheriffs was found to be difficult to arrange as they tend not to visit any one court on a regular basis and often only arrive shortly before the court is due to sit (Brown and Levy, 1998). Smaller courts allowed for the development of closer working relationships. However, social work managers cautioned against the possibility of court social workers in smaller courts being perceived by sentencers as employees of the court rather than the local authority and thus being less able to represent the interests of the social work department effectively. It was noted in McIvor and Barry (1998) that probation in the small court studied (Bruce) tended to be imposed on lower tariff offenders (in terms of the number of previous convictions and previous experience of custody) than in other courts in our sample. Thus, although one of the aims of the policy is to target probation on those most at risk of custody, in small courts there may be pressure from sentencers to target other groups of offenders.

Level of Specialisation: Service Delivery

The organisational arrangements which had been introduced across authorities were recognised by social work managers as having had an impact upon policy implementation. At the practitioner level the creation of specialist teams was said by managers and court social workers (Brown and Levy, 1998) to have enabled social workers and their immediate line managers to focus exclusively upon work with offenders and in so doing gain expertise and skills in this area of work.

Split Posts

In Scott, split posts had been created at main grade and senior social worker level. This arrangement was said by social work managers to have advantages insofar as it prevented criminal justice social workers from becoming too isolated from other areas of practice and offered a more integrated service to clients. It was also acknowledged by managers and social workers (Brown and Levy, 1998), that frustration was often felt by social workers in split posts when they were called upon to undertake urgent child protection work and managers recognised that it was difficult to ensure that time for 100 per cent funded work was adequately protected. It was believed by managers that this may have made it more difficult for staff in certain areas of work to meet the National Standards. However, the probation study (McIvor and Barry (1998) found that this area met the Standards more consistently than other more specialist areas.

One team in Scott had initially opted instead of split posts to employ three full-time criminal justice workers. Managers in this area reported that they experienced difficulties in maintaining levels and standards of service delivery in the face of staff turnover and illness, which meant that very small specialist teams were unlikely to be viable. As a result split posts were introduced, with social workers devoting varying proportions of time to intake duties. This arrangement was thought by managers in that area to work reasonably well since intake work was less likely than other forms of generic social work to encroach upon time designated for 100 per cent funded work with offenders.

Recruitment

It was suggested to a researcher in interview that enabling staff to opt for preferred specialisms rather than having a formal recruitment process had resulted, in some areas, in the appointment of staff who were not initially committed to the ethos of the National Standards. As such, the implementation of the policy at the local level was thought not to have progressed as quickly or as smoothly as it might otherwise have done.

Quality of Services

The creation of specialist posts and stability within staff groups were thought by managers and court social workers (Brown and Levy, 1998) to have been critical factors in the progress that had been made in improvements in SERs. Specialism ensured that staff had the opportunity to gain experience in SER preparation and become familiar with the National Standards to a degree that would not have been possible under generic arrangements for service delivery. Nevertheless, managers and court social workers considered that reports should be more analytic.

Managers and social workers (McAra, 1998a) thought that the quality of home circumstance reports had improved as a consequence of the National Standards. However, managers believed that these reports were not accorded sufficient priority, partly as a result of resource constraints which discouraged social workers from visiting prisoners.

Managers, social workers and sheriffs (Brown and Levy, 1998) had noted improvements in probation supervision since the shift to greater specialisation and the introduction of the National Standards. The authorities in which the greatest progress was said by managers to have been made in introducing more structured offence focused methods of probation work, were those which had the clearest specialist structures. However, as noted earlier, the area where social workers' time was not wholly allocated to criminal justice services, met the Standards more consistently than other more specialist areas (McIvor and Barry, 1998).

McIvor and Barry (1998a) found that, although community based throughcare was, in general, of limited effectiveness, there was clear evidence that the services had contributed positively to ex-prisoners' re-integration into the community and to their risk of further offending behaviour. The researchers identified factors which could improve the quality and effectiveness of community based throughcare which included: clearer objectives; more resources; and improved communication between and clarification of roles of prison based and community based social workers.

Parole Board interviewees (McAra, 1998a) had not discerned any major changes in the quality of social work services. Parole Board members identified progress in custody as the key factor when deciding on indeterminate sentence cases, which highlights the potential for prison based social work to impact on decision-making. A general view amongst social workers was that prison social work services had improved since *Continuity Through Co-operation* but that there were variations in the range and quality of services in prisons.

Managers generally agreed that the new funding arrangements had had less impact upon the quality of community service practice since community service had always been relatively efficient. In Scott, community service teams were still structurally separated from other core areas of social work criminal justice services. In Bruce and Wallace, however, steps had been taken towards the integration of community service in "generic" offender teams. In Burns, progress towards integration was said by managers to have been hampered by the fact that community service represented a "different culture" and required a "different mindset": it was found to be difficult to integrate community service as a punishment and reparation (where staff were involved in ensuring that work placements were carried out), with probation as rehabilitation, where staff worked with the offender. Those staff who administered the community service order in that area did not necessarily have a social work background.

The greatest difficulties had, however, been encountered in Wallace where the introduction of the National Standards and integration of offender services within practice teams was, managers said, viewed by community service project officers as having taken away some of the more important elements of their work. Managers in that area said that considerable attention had to be devoted by management to ensure that the resultant problems were addressed and to reassure community service staff that they had an important contribution to make.

Level of Specialisation: Management

Managers in Wallace and Burns, which had specialist structures to middle or senior level, believed that these arrangements had served to protect the interests of criminal justice social work and had facilitated the implementation of the policy. In Scott and Bruce, where generic structures had been introduced for operational management above the level of senior social worker or practice team manager, potential difficulties were acknowledged by managers to exist through the separation of strategic and operational management functions.

The organisational structure that had been developed in the region in which Bruce was located, was described by managers in that area as having both advantages and disadvantages. On the positive side, the creation of a separate strategic planning and co-ordination function had facilitated the development of expertise in planning and provided a focus for liaison between the authority and the Scottish Office. On the other hand, however, the lack of operational management responsibility on the part of the lead officer for offender services created difficulties in improving the standards of service on a consistent basis across the authority. This had to be achieved by indirect means such as through feedback, reports and discussion. Generic managers at the local level were said to vary in terms of their interest and expertise in criminal justice work with the result that the level and quality of support for specialist staff varied from district to district

In Scott, the lead officer for offender services had no direct line management responsibility for the work undertaken by area teams. This was said by managers in that area to have inhibited the amount of contact with area team staff and, as in Bruce, made it more difficult to ensure that the policy was implemented on a consistent basis across the district.

CO-ORDINATING CRIMINAL JUSTICE AND COMMUNITY CARE POLICIES

It was considered by Main Consultation Group respondents that arrangements for co-ordinating policies for those who were users of criminal justice and other social work services, were inadequate (for example, linking criminal justice work and child abuse, links between criminal justice and community care planning, and links between social work, health and criminal justice for services for mentally disordered offenders). It was recognised that there was a need to adopt a coherent approach and to encourage networking. One Main Consultant Group respondent considered that the required models had not yet been identified but others believed that the Standards and planning arrangements allowed priorities to be identified and should provide a structure within which deficiencies could be addressed.

Some Main Consultation Group respondents suggested that, although joint social work/community care plans linked with the interests of the health board, in practice these links did not always operate effectively and that with changes in personnel, the implementation of policy and strategy could be quite difficult. Lack of progress in co-ordinating policies could, they suggested, be due to a lack of resources and the priority of particular types of offenders:

> "There is a need to lay the foundations of the service as a whole before attention can be focused on particular policy areas, care groups and subsets of offenders because these offenders, their problems and problems in co-ordination and networking are very complex and are cost intensive. There is a tension between that and the principle of the greatest amount of good for the greatest number of people, which has been dominant up until now, but space is now beginning to be created for focusing on subgroups although the pace is affected by the availability of resources." (MCG2)

In the area of substance misuse, some Main Consultation Group representatives reported that work was progressing linking the requirements of effective social work practice within criminal justice services with access to resources within community care, although it was suggested that alcohol misuse had a lower profile than drug misuse.

Some managers considered that although 100 per cent funding had speeded the development of specialisation, criminal justice staff felt deskilled in other areas of work and that this problem should be addressed to ensure they take a wider view of the family and the needs of the mentally disordered offender. There were considered by some Main Consultation Group respondents to be risks attached to having a too rigid specialist hierarchy and a belief was expressed that specialisms should be better integrated.

Within each authority managers reported that a variety of mechanisms had been introduced to ensure that criminal justice services were adequately represented at different levels of the organisation and integrated with other social work services. In Burns, criminal justice services had been subsumed under the community care management structure at senior level. Regular meetings were held between different heads of service and between managers of criminal justice, community care and child care teams. The generic management structure that had been developed in Bruce was said by managers in that area to represent a conscious attempt to integrate social work services at middle and senior management level. Whilst managers thought integration had been reasonably effective at these levels, regular meetings between specialist practice team managers were said by some senior managers to have been characterised, in one district at least, by a propensity to draw boundaries between different areas of service delivery.

In Scott, links between senior managers of different services were described by those managers interviewed as networks rather than formal structures, though criminal justice interests were represented at directorate level by the depute director with responsibility for this area of service delivery. At a local level district co-ordinators for offender services had formal arrangements for liaison with colleagues in child care and community care. One of the benefits of the structural separation of services was thought by managers to have been the development of more effective, formal systems for liaison across different specialisms. In Wallace, a number of different strategic planning groups had been developed and criminal justice managers were involved in any policy or planning discussions in which offender issues featured.

None of the authorities had established explicit guidance on determining which specialist area should have responsibility for cases which straddled different specialisms. Instead there was an expectation in each authority that statutory work with offenders would be undertaken by specialist criminal justice staff unless there were good practice reasons for doing otherwise. Such decisions tended to be made on a case-by-case basis with the interests of the offender featuring prominently as the primary criterion for determining who should assume responsibility for the work. The number of these cases per year was low and managers did not consider this issue to be problematic.

THE IMPACT OF FUNDING ON SERVICE PROVISION

100 Per Cent Funded Services

In 1993, the research on early arrangements (McAra, 1998) identified a tension in the policy between the framework of the National Standards and the need to develop services within available resources. This tension was still apparent in 1995. As noted earlier, local authority plans and social work managers reported difficulties in obtaining funding for the development of existing services and the introduction of new initiatives. Court social workers and social workers in three study areas considered that there were insufficient substance misuse services to meet demand and gaps in service provision were identified in most areas, for example supported accommodation for offenders (Brown and Levy, 1998) and (McAra, 1998a). Social workers considered that where there were waiting lists for services such as sex offender programmes, this could impact adversely on parole decisions (McAra, 1998a).

Throughcare was considered by Main Consultation interviewees and managers to be an area that was still under developed, despite local authority plans identifying this service as a priority. Community based throughcare was acknowledged by managers to be the area in which the least progress had been made in terms of policy implementation. They considered it to be the area in which the greatest difficulty had been encountered in meeting National Standards, partly because it was particularly resource intensive on account of the travel costs and staff time involved in visiting prisoners located in institutions across the country. Some social workers suggested that the lack of necessary resources had limited the effectiveness of community-based throughcare provision (McIvor and Barry, 1998a).

The existence in Scott of a dedicated throughcare project, funded through the Urban Renewal Unit, was said by managers to have provided a more efficient and effective throughcare service for serving prisoners. McIvor and Barry, (1998a) found that, in respect of the timing of initial interviews and frequency of contacts with ex-prisoners following release, the National Standards were being met more consistently in Scott than in other areas.

Managers and Main Consultation Group interviewees considered that the separate funding mechanism of prison based social work had impacted adversely on the creation of an effective integrated throughcare service partly because of the relative priority which prison management attributed to the service. Some prison social work units were, it was suggested, not receiving sufficient resources to allow policy objectives to be achieved. These views were consistent with the findings of the inspection (SWSI, 1993).

Non 100 Per Cent Funded Services

Early concerns expressed at a Main Consultation Group meeting in 1993[13] that insufficient priority had been given to services which were not 100 per cent funded, in particular diversion, were still evident during interviews conducted in 1995. Some Main Consultation Group respondents stated that, given local authority expenditure constraints, authorities could not realistically be expected to expand non-100 per cent services, whereas others pointed out that a lot of innovative work takes place in that area. Social work managers believed that the fact that certain services had not been brought under the umbrella of 100 per cent funding had prevented authorities from developing a comprehensive network of social work criminal justice services.

Diversion to social work was an area which managers in each of the authorities would have wished to develop on a more formal basis. In most areas ad hoc arrangements were in place to enable procurators fiscal to divert cases where appropriate but authorities had been unable to extend the existing level of provision. Managers in smaller authorities in particular said that they had insufficient scope and flexibility within regional budgets to provide financial support for more than a limited diversion service. Lack of funding was not, however, the only impediment to offering pre-prosecution diversion to social work on a larger scale. To do so would require the active support and co-operation of procurators fiscal and in some areas procurators fiscal were said to have shown no interest in the development of a formal diversion scheme. This being the case, greater uniformity of provision is unlikely to be achieved in the absence of central guidance within the procurator fiscal service that procurators fiscal should enter into formal agreements with local authorities and divert appropriate cases from prosecution.

In one area, management indicated that had work undertaken with offenders on deferred sentences been eligible for 100 per cent funding "we might have adopted a slightly different strategy in relation to probation". Services related to monetary penalties were also thought to have suffered under the new funding arrangements, with some managers believing that this area of work received "if anything less attention than before because it's clearly not a priority".

Range of Service Providers

Most representatives of the Main Consultation Group believed that the policy had increased the range of organisations involved in providing services to the criminal justice system, and that the initiative had allowed independent organisations to develop services to the criminal justice system. However, some Main Consultation Group representatives commented that the range of organisations providing services had grown more slowly than expected, that there was still a need to develop more community based interventions, and that the potential for networking services at the local level had not been sufficiently exploited. This view was supported by findings about early arrangements (McAra, 1998) which found that the National Standards were considered to have had minimal impact on the development of specialist schemes, especially those aimed at

---

[13] Minutes of the meeting of Main Consultation Group, November 1993.

young people involved in less serious offences. Table 3.1 also shows that few specialised services were introduced in the study areas after 1992. Independent sector providers suggested that agencies which depended largely on 100 per cent funding found it difficult to develop initiatives which did not qualify for 100 per cent funding, unless an initiative was funded on a pilot basis.

The four study authorities made varying use of independent sector provision to extend the range of locally available services (Table 3.1). Scott made least use of services provided by the independent sector (two out of the four specialist services available) primarily because the majority of services, such as intensive probation for high tariff probationers, were provided directly by the local authority. The three specialist services in Bruce were all provided by the independent sector. Managers acknowledged that there was more opportunity within larger authorities to earmark regional funding for the development of more specialised services to offenders. Wallace and Burns had the greatest number of specialist services (seven and six respectively), each having five specialist services provided by the independent sector.

TRAINING

The Scottish Office has promoted training (SWSI, 1993) by: recognising training requirements within 100 per cent funding; making funds available to the Central Council for Education and Training in Social Work (CCETSW) to prepare guidance for courses, making funds available to establish a joint programme for criminal justice, social work management and practice involving Edinburgh and Stirling universities; and supporting the development of National Vocational Qualification/ Scottish Vocational Qualification courses and a course in management at Jordanhill College.

A comprehensive training needs analysis had been conducted in only one of the four authorities. Managers had mixed views as to how effective centrally determined training strategies had been. Whilst some believed that they had been effective and that attempts had been made to involve staff at different levels of the organisation in identifying training needs, others suggested that it had failed to be responsive to the needs of staff at the local level.

It was evident from strategic plans and from interviews with social work managers that the types of training provided to staff had evolved during the period of time since the introduction of 100 per cent funding. It ranged from broadly based induction training aimed at familiarising staff with the requirements of the National Standards, to a greater focus upon training aimed at the acquisition of more advanced skills or of skills in more specialised areas of work.

All managers were aware of the need for staff to receive further training in particular areas - work with sex offenders, substance misusers and mentally disordered offenders were those most often mentioned. Court social workers (Brown and Levy, 1998) also identified a need for further improvements in providing more analytic assessments in SERs, which could be met through training. By and large managers believed that the amount and type of training provided had been adequate and appropriate to the needs of the organisation.

LOCAL GOVERNMENT REORGANISATION

Range of Services

Local government reorganisation was acknowledged as being likely to impact significantly upon the provision of social work services in the criminal justice system. Particular concern was expressed in respect of smaller authorities which, it was recognised, would be unable, unless they contracted with other authorities, to offer a comprehensive range of services to offenders and their families because of diseconomies of scale. Reorganisation was seen by Scottish Office representatives as requiring the creation of a much more collaborative approach to providing and developing services and support functions such as training.

The judicial interviewees in the present study and in the study on sentencer decision making were concerned that criminal justice social work services might not continue to receive the same level of priority and commitment and that the full range of services might not be available. This, they said, would limit the options in the case of each offender and the risk of custody might become greater.

> "It would be a great sadness if we went back to that." (MCG1)

Management

The difficulty of managing smaller budgets would, social work managers suggested, preclude the flexibility which currently existed in the larger authorities to meet the costs of services that were not subject to 100 per cent funding. Scottish Office interviewees were concerned that, although senior local authority management would remain conversant with and committed to criminal justice services, their responsibilities might be more widely spread which would restrict the time available to devote to developing innovation. Managers considered that criminal justice social work staff in smaller authorities would also suffer from a loss of peer and management support and would have less opportunity to develop expertise across a broad range of criminal justice work, while new authorities in general would lose the "sense of wider strategy" that was possible within larger social work departments.

Independent Sector

One benefit of the creation of single tier authorities would be to make social work services more responsive to locally defined needs and to bring the local authority and the independent sector closer together with a sense of common purpose. Some social work managers expressed concern, however, that smaller authorities in particular would be characterised by greater political interference in response to public opinion. Councils might, it was argued by managers, be unwilling to meet the costs of providing services for which full central government funding was not available to an 'unpopular client group'.

Local government reorganisation was thought likely to have a greater impact upon the independent sector which would be required to contract with a larger number of authorities to maintain existing levels of service provision. Some concern was expressed that independent sector organisations would be discouraged from providing services to smaller, predominantly rural, authorities which would be unable to offer economies of scale. Independent sector service providers acknowledged that they would have to be more flexible in terms of service delivery and while some also saw reorganisation as presenting positive challenges and opportunities, the necessity of dealing with a larger number of authorities might, it was suggested, preclude the development of such close working relationships between the two sectors as had begun to be evidenced over recent years.

Liaison

Liaison with criminal justice agencies would also become more complex with, for instance, some small authorities straddling two or more sheriffdoms and most sheriffdoms being served by a larger number of authorities. The development of an integrated throughcare strategy would be further complicated and prison social work units would become more vulnerable under the new arrangements.

Organisational Structures

Some social work managers believed that there was a risk of returning to generic models of service delivery in rural authorities where pressures existed to deliver devolved services to communities. Should this occur, one manager suggested that 'criminal justice will go to the bottom of the pile and there will be a loss of skills and specialist knowledge'. More generally, social work managers expressed hope that the new authorities would be willing to work together to preserve the experience and expertise that had accrued over the years following the implementation of the policy.

CONCLUSION

Local policy implementation, in particular the quality of SERs and probation supervision, was viewed by managers and court social workers (Brown and Levy, 1998) to have been enhanced by the national requirement for the creation of specialist arrangements for service delivery. However, it was found that such arrangements could not be sustained without a certain degree of centralisation at the local level: very small teams of specialist workers were particularly vulnerable to the consequences of staff turnover and illness. Specialist management structures appeared better suited than generic arrangements to ensure a consistent level and standard of policy implementation across an authority.

The implementation of community care policy appeared to have impacted negatively upon criminal justice services at the local level, especially in those departments with generic management structures. The restructuring of departments to accommodate criminal justice and community care policy implementation was said by managers to have served to compartmentalise different social work services and that staff felt deskilled in other areas of work. This was said by managers to have delayed the development of mechanisms at management and practitioner level to integrate policy and practice across different specialist areas. At the national level, Main Consultation Group interviewees identified a need to integrate service provision and co-ordinate policies.

The policy objective of providing an adequate supply of services had not been fully achieved. Although a few specialist services had been introduced in the study areas since 1991, managers, local authority plans and some sheriffs identified gaps in service provision in respect of the range and number of available places of specialist services. This was partly attributed to the lack of funding. The provision of throughcare services was seen by interviewees to have suffered through the lack of resources and because of the separate funding mechanism of prison based social work. Rural areas were said to have experienced difficulties in accessing or providing specialist services because of the relatively low level of demand. In addition offenders were often reluctant to attend services outwith their local environment.

Managers said that insufficient priority had been given to services which were not 100 per cent funded such as diversion, and that this had prevented authorities from developing a comprehensive network of services.

CHAPTER FOUR
REVIEW OF POLICY IMPLEMENTATION

INTRODUCTION

When the National Standards were introduced in 1991, it was agreed that a rolling programme of reviews of the various parts of the Standards would be necessary in the light of experience and in response to changes in legislation. Guidelines are also developed to coincide with the introduction of new initiatives which are 100 per cent funded and these are later upgraded to National Standards. (Annex I indicates which standards have been, or are, in the process of being reviewed).

Although the initiative for much of this work comes from SWSG, the reviews and revisions are carried out by National Standards Review Groups which comprise representatives from a wide range of criminal justice interests, but these are not set up as subgroups of the Main Consultation Group. The function of these groups is to prepare draft standards or revise existing Standards and to produce a report on any relevant issues such as proposals for legislative revision. Although not subject to detailed oversight or approval by the Main Consultation Group, the results of these National Standards Review Groups are reported to the Group at its annual meeting as part of the process of external consultation which also includes issue of draft Standards to a wide range of key stakeholders for comment.

In identifying Standards which should be revised and considering how improvements can be achieved, SWSG and the Standards Review Groups rely on feedback from key stakeholders in the criminal justice system (including the Main Consultation Group) and on feedback from inspections undertaken by SWSI on the progress of implementation. SWSI undertake this task by a programme of inspection visits and visits to review financial arrangements.

Monitoring and evaluation are necessary at the local level to assist in the improvement of the quality of services and in identifying needs for services. At the national level, they are required to assess the extent to which the policy has been implemented and to identify areas where further guidance is required. The programme of review and development therefore depends on having effective mechanisms for monitoring and evaluation and national consultation. The purpose of this chapter is to assess the effectiveness of those mechanisms in relation to the monitoring, evaluation and review of policy implementation and development.

MONITORING AND EVALUATION

From April 1991 central government has been required to monitor and evaluate the management and delivery of the 100 per cent funded social work services. SWSG's strategy comprises a professional and financial audit of services and a programme of research. The audit comprises: an analysis of statistical material; a programme of inspection visits by SWSI; and periodic visits to review financial arrangements. For their part, local authorities have been required to provide Central Government with statistical returns and information necessary to review: the organisation, management and delivery of services; the national objectives, priorities and standards; the funding arrangements; and legislation. Local authorities are also required to monitor local compliance with national objectives, priorities and standards and evaluate the extent to which services are being managed and delivered effectively, efficiently and economically.

National Core Data System (NCDS)

The Standards state that SWSG is responsible for the creation and maintenance of a NCDS as a key element of its evaluation strategy and as a basis for its analysis of statistical material. The detailed form and content of the NCDS was determined by SWSG in consultation with COSLA and other interested parties: local authorities are required to complete returns to SWSG on SERs, and community service and probation order termination reports. The analysis of these returns may be complemented with national criminal justice statistics. The system was designed to support :

- an analysis of the impact of national objectives, priorities and standards on the level of custody and the use of community based social work disposals and services.
- national and local oversight of service provision including compliance with National Standards, resource planning and quality control.

It was originally intended that the NCDS would be fully operational and tested by Spring 1993 but a series of problems, such as a high level of data errors, delayed its full operation. It was suggested by Main Consultation Group representatives that the original data coverage was too ambitious and that there was some confusion over the aims of the NCDS.

A subgroup of the COSLA/SWSG Organisation and Management Group was convened in 1995 to review the NCDS. As a result, the format of local authority returns were revised and piloted in 1996. The Scottish Office representatives interviewed acknowledged the delay in providing feedback to local authorities but said that the review of the NCDS should resolve that problem: in future, the system would be driven by the needs of the local authorities and Central Government would collect aggregated data. The independent sector were unhappy that they were unable to access the system.

Each of the local authorities in the study areas had dedicated research and information staff who were responsible for developing and implementing information systems to facilitate monitoring and evaluation of services. Although all authorities had made progress in implementing comprehensive information systems, difficulties were encountered in the development of systems which were compatible with existing information systems whilst at the same time providing information required by the NCDS. The delay in implementing computerised information systems was acknowledged to have impacted negatively upon the effectiveness of the planning process.

Social work managers expressed disappointment that the NCDS was not yet producing the information it was intended to provide and that it had made no contribution to the review and planning of services at the local level.

Scottish Office Statistics

The criminal justice statistics produced by The Scottish Office, and particularly those relating to sentencing patterns across courts, were considered by social work managers to be of some value. The Scottish Office representatives agreed that Home Department criminal justice statistics were useful for national and local planning, targeting of resources and in allowing trends to be identified and as such providing background information for service development.

However, social work managers and independent sector providers had some reservations, for example: the community service SWSG statistical report for 1993 was viewed by managers as a summary which 'told you nothing' (Social Work Manager); statistics were published without advanced notice and lacked adequate commentary; and there was too long a delay in their production. It was suggested that certain types of information that might assist in planning and service development were missing, for example, the number of those remanded who subsequently received a non-custodial sentence.

SWSI Inspections

The inspections assess the extent to which national objectives, priorities and standards for centrally funded services are being economically, efficiently and effectively implemented by local authorities and other agencies and identify any need for change in the way these services are organised, managed and delivered[14]. Reviews of local authority organisational and management systems normally form part of the programme of inspections.

Social work managers indicated that they had not found inspections useful in planning and service development, primarily because of the time which had elapsed between the inspection visit and production of a report. For this reason they found informal feedback at the time of inspection to be more useful. Some managers felt that inspections focused on negative points, were superficial and told authorities 'nothing we didn't already know'. However, managers did welcome the concept of inspection both as a means of focusing upon issues that require attention and as an exercise in accountability.

Mechanisms for monitoring the quality of services

Local Authority Services

A variety of methods had been developed by authorities to monitor the quality of social work services subject to 100 per cent funding. At the most basic level, staff supervision was regarded by managers as a useful mechanism for monitoring the quality of services provided, though its effectiveness was questioned if

---

[14] In 1996, SWSI's statement of purpose and responsibilities changed to: "Our purpose is to work with others to continually improve social work services so that: they genuinely meet people's needs; and the public has confidence in them."

immediate line managers had generic responsibility and little interest or expertise in work with offenders. Probation and throughcare reviews likewise provided an opportunity for some managers to monitor the quality of ongoing work with clients as did, in one authority, the occasional examination of case files by a senior manager.

Three of the authorities had introduced continuous sampling procedures to ensure that social enquiry reports were consistent with the National Standards. A similar annual exercise, based on samples of cases, was undertaken in Scott in relation to probation supervision, community service and throughcare services. In addition to identifying areas in which practice could, in general, be improved, the results of these exercises were discussed with individual social workers who, despite concerns on the part of management that staff might find the process threatening, apparently valued the feedback provided. However, in one authority individual feedback had been met with resistance by staff and had been replaced by a system of anonymised sampling.

Computerised information was also used to examine conversion of SER recommendations to disposals and in two authorities all SERs which were followed by a custodial outcome were monitored to identify any relevant trends. An SER support group had been established in one team to assist less experienced staff in putting together supervision packages to present to the court.

Whilst significant progress had been made in most authorities to monitor the quality of services, less emphasis had been placed upon the development of methods to evaluate the effectiveness of social work services in the criminal justice system. This was particularly true in respect of one-to-one work undertaken in the context of mainstream services such as probation supervision and throughcare; less so in relation to more specialised, group based programmes of intervention. Wallace had made funding available for an independent evaluation of its sex offender treatment programme whilst the intensive probation programme provided by Scott was also the subject of independent evaluative research. On a less formal basis evaluative methods, such as the use of exit questionnaires, were commonly used by practitioners to assess the effectiveness of group work provision but were only employed on a routine basis in Scott to obtain feedback on the perceived helpfulness of individual supervision.

Non-Local Authority Provision

One difficulty that had been encountered by some authorities related to the monitoring of additional requirements to the probation order and, in particular, ensuring that specialist agencies, such as mental health professionals or substance misuse counselling services, were meeting the National Standards with respect to enforcement. Independent sector providers were able to describe mechanisms for the monitoring and evaluation of services which they provided. Three projects were subject to independent external evaluation which was supplemented by internal monitoring through the use of computerised data bases. Other mechanisms for monitoring service provision included the production of annual reports, the preparation of regular statistical summaries for the local authority and regional inspections.

Various opportunities arose for independent sector providers to discuss with local authorities changes to or improvements in service delivery. On a formal level annual meetings with social work managers provided a vehicle for reviewing services and discussing proposals for changes. Less formally, however, all independent sector providers were able to instigate meetings with the local authority on an ad hoc basis as and when required to discuss potential developments at the strategic or operational level.

Prison based social work

Systems for monitoring and evaluating the effectiveness of prison based social work services were thought by Main Consultation Group representatives and managers to be less well developed. Although managers in two authorities said that they had introduced computerised systems in their prison social work units, these were said to be less effective than the systems that had been introduced to monitor community based services. This was essentially because the information provided by them was more limited and 'more concerned with outputs or numbers than with the effectiveness of the services provided'. Although some prison based group work programmes had been subject to evaluation, inspection was said to have been the main vehicle for monitoring the quality of services provided by prison based social work units in one authority while prison social work management plans were said to have served a similar function in another region.

REVIEW

The need to establish a formal process of annual review of policy and priorities which would encompass the feedback from each of the National Standards Review Groups, was first identified in 1993 at meetings of the COSLA/SWSG Strategic Planning Review Group (which was established to review the planning section of the National Standards) and the Main Consultation Group. Social Work Services Group explained that it was considering ways of improving contribution to policy development within the criminal justice system. Respondents considered that the need still existed for the development of a strategic overview of policy and priorities, addressing issues such as services not within the 100 per cent funding; the needs of mentally disturbed offenders; identifying priorities such as the development of accommodation services against the development of supervised attendance orders; the relationship between the local authority and the independent sector; and an examination of the relationship between provision of community disposals and their impact on prison numbers.

Main Consultation Group respondents proposed certain criteria for undertaking an effective overview of policy and priorities. Some suggested that it was necessary to develop networks, both at the national and local level, by holding specific discussions with individual groups (similar to the meeting between SWSG and the Sheriffs' Association and quarterly meetings between SWSG and representatives of the independent sector), and by a national group of stakeholders linking with those responsible for policy in areas such as employment, housing and the police, which would facilitate the development, acquisition and use of resources to underpin practice as distinct from the development of Standards.

The potential mechanism for review of policy implementation and development is the Main Consultation Group. The original role of the Main Consultation Group was the preparation and design of the National Standards (1991). At interview, representatives of the Main Consultation Group identified the current role of the Group as being to monitor the development of the Standards by providing a forum in which those from different perspectives could share their experiences and views of policy implementation and to act as a 'sounding board' for new ideas.

However, the Group was constrained in the review of policy implementation by a number of factors. It was suggested that the lack of comparative national statistical information inhibited identification of the more subtle indicators of success of implementation and views could be swayed by occasional instances of poor practice presented at meetings. Although the Group had discussed sentencing patterns at the most recent meeting (1995), it was acknowledged that a review of policy requiring detailed monitoring of policy implementation comparing sentencing patterns with performance of social work departments, would be delayed until information bases in performance and performance indicators had been developed.

Main Consultation Group respondents considered that the Group's work in the review of policy implementation was also constrained by the infrequency of meetings. This was seen to inhibit the maintenance of the role of overseeing policy implementation other than receiving progress reports; the ability to undertake detailed monitoring of policy implementation; the ability to make rapid progress; and the development of a more strategic and proactive role. In its present format, it was suggested that the Group could not effectively undertake the role of a rigorous oversight of policy implementation.

Some Main Consultation Group respondents considered that the Group was in a transitionary phase and that its future role should be reconsidered within the wider context of the needs of the next phase of development of the policy. Main Consultation Group interviewees suggested that the membership of the Group should be reconsidered and that frequency of meetings be increased to increase its effectiveness and influence but that it would not become involved in detailed work, which would be undertaken by subgroups or separate working groups.[15] Proposals by Main Consultation Group respondents for the future role of the Group included: agreeing the annual statement of priorities; considering which standards ought to be revised; and considering the impact of local government reorganisation.

It is evident that maintaining a strategic overview of the policy would require extensive effort by working groups in order to obtain national feedback from interest groups and analyse national information on monitoring and evaluation. Some Main Consultation Group respondents suggested that membership of such groups should include each organisation with an interest in or providing criminal justice services. These groups could be established as subgroups of the Main Consultation Group or could constitute a taskforce reporting to a Scottish Office interdepartmental group which would present draft reports to the Main Consultation Group for comment.

---

[15] The fieldwork for the study was completed in March 1993. The minutes of the November 1993 meeting of the Main Consultation Group indicate that the issue of more frequent meetings was raised but that members decided to continue to meet on an annual basis.

CONCLUSION

The delay in fully implementing the NCDS inhibited local planning and a national review of implementation of the policy. However, the review of the NCDS and revised proforma were intended to provide a more effective national information system. Scottish Office criminal justice statistics were viewed as helpful by managers but the delay in their publication and that of inspections reduced their value in the local planning process.

It was evident that there was a need for a strategic overview of the implementation and development of the policy. Although the role of the Main Consultation Group was to monitor the progress of implementation of the Standards, some members interviewed suggested that the operation of the Group did not facilitate effective monitoring or a strategic overview of policy implementation.

Some Main Consultation Group representatives suggested that, in order to provide a strategic overview of policy implementation and development, either the Main Consultation Group should be reconvened to encompass more focused representation of key groups, or a separate group should be established. They proposed that such a group should meet more frequently to be able to meet the demands of the task and should be informed by a more rigorous system of obtaining national feedback on policy implementation, based on effective national consultation and on effective national monitoring and evaluation.

CHAPTER FIVE
KEY ISSUES AND CONCLUSIONS

INTRODUCTION

The purpose of this study is to describe the national and local context within which the policy was developed, implemented and reviewed prior to and during the period within which the research programme was conducted. Views obtained from representatives of the Main Consultation Group and Scottish Office documents provide an assessment of policy implementation at the national level, and local government documents and views of social work managers, court social workers and social workers provide a view of policy implementation at the local level.

The following discussion summarises the findings in respect of: consultation; planning and funding; organisational structures; and monitoring.

CONSULTATION

National consultation, which is conducted primarily through the Main Consultation Group, was generally seen by those members interviewed, to have been effective in involving key stakeholders in developing the National Standards and generating a sense of ownership of them.

The Judiciary

Some Main Consultation Group interviewees suggested that the Group could have approached the judiciary for more assistance in raising awareness of policy implementation and in the pursuit of a more coherent judicial response to the development of services. At the local level, interviews with sheriffs and social work managers indicated that formal liaison with the judiciary did not always take place in all of the study areas and where this existed, it was not always effective. Some sheriffs, however, were reluctant to participate in formal liaison but identified a need for more information on the performance of offenders and success of orders. Such information could be provided at formal liaison meetings. Informal liaison, in particular between sheriffs and court social workers, was viewed by them to be operating well.

Procurators Fiscal

Some Main Consultation Group respondents considered that the proposed inclusion of diversion within 100 per cent funding had given impetus to the development of links with procurators fiscal and to the development of more coherent systems for interacting with court agencies. Although managers reported that formal arrangements had been introduced in two areas, liaison was generally conducted on an informal level. Managers and those procurators fiscal who were interviewed considered that existing liaison arrangements were satisfactory.

Prisons

At the national level, liaison between SPS and social work criminal justice services could, some Main Consultation Group representatives believed, be more effective. In addition they, and the findings of the inspection (SWSI, 1993), indicated that liaison between community based and prison based social workers could be improved. At the local level, whilst liaison between social work departments and prisons within their boundaries were seen to be satisfactory, managers considered that the absence of formal mechanisms for cross-boundary liaison could be compounded by the creation of a larger number of smaller authorities following local government reorganisation.

Independent Sector

At the national level, networks between local authorities and the independent sector could, some Main Consultation Group members believed, have been exploited to a greater extent. However, at the local level, social work managers and independent sector providers in the study areas considered that, in general, the nature and extent of liaison had been adequate. Nevertheless, they recognised that some factors had, where they existed, possibly prevented relationships from being more productive: the absence of service agreements; a lack of regular contact with social work teams to ensure a constant flow of referrals; staff turnover in the local authority; and the lack of a joint forum for joint discussion of strategic issues. However, the National Standards were considered by managers and independent sector providers as having facilitated good liaison arrangements which resulted in greater accountability.

PLANNING AND FUNDING

Planning

The planning process was seen by managers to have engendered a greater sense of ownership of service and policy objectives amongst practitioners and to have disciplined authorities to conduct internal reviews consistent throughout Scotland. The planning process was believed by managers to have contributed positively to the development of services by providing a focus for the development of services and establishment of priorities within an overall objective.

Interviewees and documents reported that the preliminary planning procedures, introduced on a national level, did not operate effectively at the local level and that absence of reliable statistical information at both the national and local levels hindered planning. Steps have been taken to remedy these problems: revised planning procedures have been introduced and the system for providing national information has been reviewed.

Managers, sheriffs and social workers identified a need for a wider range of specialist services and an increased quantity of available places. Interviewees reported that rural areas experienced particular difficulties in accessing or providing services. The absence of a sufficient number of places or an appropriate specialist service could, some sheriffs argued, dissuade them from imposing a non-custodial sentence in some cases. If the courts' needs for services are not met, this could inhibit the achievement of policy objectives.

Main Consultation Group respondents and managers believed that a more collaborative approach to providing and developing services would be required with smaller authorities following local government reorganisation as smaller authorities would be unable on their own to offer a comprehensive range of services because of diseconomies of scale. This, managers believed, might discourage the independent sector from providing services to smaller, predominantly rural, authorities. Sheriffs were concerned that the full range of services might not be available which would limit the options in each case and the risk of custody might thus become greater.

Funding

The study of early arrangements which was conducted in 1993 (McAra, 1998), identified a tension between the framework of the National Standards and the need to develop services within available resources. This tension was still apparent during the fieldwork of this study. Managers and local authority plans expressed concern about obtaining an appropriate level of funding to develop existing services, establish additional specialist services and introduce more innovative methods of work. In general, managers highlighted the need to prioritise carefully to ensure that standards in the core areas of service delivery were met, which might be at the expense of introducing more innovative and potentially more effective methods of work.

Throughcare was considered by Main Consultation Group interviewees and managers to be an area that was still under developed, despite local authority plans identifying this as an area of priority. Reasons for the slow progress in developing throughcare provided by managers and some Main Consultation Group interviewees included: the relative priority which prison management attributed to the service; the separate funding of social work in prisons; it is resource intensive on account of travel costs and staff time; and the relatively low number of offenders receiving throughcare services.

Managers and interviewees in the study of early arrangements (McAra, 1998) believed that availability of 100 per cent funding had protected core services. Managers believed that the development of a comprehensive approach to planning and service delivery was hindered by the absence of 100 per cent funding for some services such as diversion. Managers suggested that the difficulty of managing smaller budgets might preclude the flexibility which currently existed in larger authorities to meet the costs of services not subject to 100 per cent funding.

ORGANISATIONAL STRUCTURES

A range of organisational structures had been adopted by the four study areas: from specialist offender services teams to teams in which social workers spent part of their time on other services (Scott); and from generic to specialist middle and senior management.

The shift to greater specialisation and the introduction of the National Standards were viewed by managers, court social workers and some sheriffs, as having resulted in improvements in the preparation of SERs and probation. However, McIvor and Barry (1978) found that the National Standards were most closely met in the area whose teams were less specialised. On the other hand, managers considered that the areas in which the greatest progress had been made in introducing more structured offence focused methods of probation work, were those which had the clearest specialist structures. Brown and Levy (1998) found that the quality of SERs did not differ significantly between the study areas.

Some social work managers believed that there was a risk of returning to generic models of service delivery in rural authorities where pressures existed to deliver devolved services to communities. Managers considered that specialist staff in smaller authorities might suffer from a loss of peer and management support and would have less opportunity to develop expertise across a broad range of criminal justice work.

MONITORING

Whilst in most authorities significant progress had been made in monitoring the quality of services, less emphasis had been placed upon the development of methods to evaluate services, in particular one-to-one work with offenders. In addition, difficulties had been encountered by some authorities in monitoring additional requirements to probation orders and ensuring that specialist agencies were meeting the National Standards in respect of enforcement.

Systems for monitoring and evaluating the effectiveness of prison based social work services were thought by Main Consultation Group interviewees and managers to be less well developed.

Interviewees acknowledged that the delay in fully implementing the National Core Data System (NCDS) had hindered local planning and a national review of policy implementation. However, steps had been taken to review the system. The delay in publication of Scottish Office criminal justice statistics and results of inspections were considered by managers to have reduced their value in the local planning process.

Main Consultation Group respondents identified a need for the development of a strategic overview of policy and priorities but acknowledged that the Group did not meet sufficiently frequently to undertake a rigorous review of policy implementation at a national level.

CONCLUSION

The research was conducted in the early stages of policy implementation and thus some aspects of implementation were not complete. Certain aspects of implementation at the national level facilitated local policy implementation:

- The involvement of key stakeholders in the preparation of the National Standards.
- The national planning process enhanced local planning by providing a focus for development and establishment of priorities.

Other aspects of national implementation hindered local implementation:

- The absence of 100 per cent funding for all services hindered the development of a comprehensive approach to planning and service delivery.
- Sufficient funding was not made available to provide the full range and level of specialist services identified as being required in local plans.
- Early planning procedures were not found to be totally effective and these have since been revised.
- The delay in establishing an effective National Core Data System and delays in providing feedback of national statistics and findings of inspections hindered national and local reviews of policy implementation.
- The separate funding and priority allocated to social work in prisons was seen by some interviewees to have partly attributed to the slow progress in developing throughcare services.

ANNEX I

PREPARATION AND REVISION OF NATIONAL STANDARDS AND GUIDELINES

Community Service	National Standards (revised in 1994)
Throughcare	National Standards (revised in 1996)
Probation	National Standards 1991
Supervised Attendance	National Guidelines 1992 (Standards due 1998)
Diversion from Prosecution	National Guidelines 1994
Supervised Release Orders/ Prison Based Social Work	Interim Guidance 1995 (Incorporated into 1996 Throughcare National Standards)
Supported Accommodation	Interim Guidance 1995 (Standards due 1998)
Bail Information and Supervision	Interim Guidance 1995 (Standards under consideration)
Imprisonment and Preparation for Release of Offenders Convicted of Offences against Children	National Guidelines 1994 (Incorporated into 1996 Throughcare National Standard)
Strategic Planning	National Standards (revised in 1996)

ANNEX II

PLANNING PRINCIPLES

The National Standards laid down general principles to be followed in the development and maintenance of local planning systems. The plans should:

(i) have as their main focus, the application of national objectives, priorities and standards to the circumstances prevailing in individual regional authorities;

(ii) show what is trying to be achieved across the range of social work services in the criminal justice system, with the emphasis on the type and level of planned action to improve the range, quality and targeting of services, and on identifiable outcomes;

(iii) be based on consultation and liaison with other local authority departments, the judiciary, other agencies in the criminal justice system and relevant independent sector agencies;

(iv) be aligned with policy planning for other services provided by the social work departments for people in need;

(v) be capable of providing sufficient scope for local initiatives and imaginative and flexible use of resources in response to local conditions;

(vi) be informed by evidence drawn from management information systems to assist policy planning and review, quality assurance, the monitoring of performance and evaluation of service outcomes;

(vii) include reference to staff induction and in-service training programmes which ensure that staff have the knowledge and competence to carry out their responsibilities to required standards.

REFERENCES

Brown, L. and Levy L. (1998) *Social Work and Criminal Justice: Sentencer Decision Making*. Edinburgh: The Stationery Office.

COSLA/SWSG Strategic Planning Review Group. Minutes of meetings held between November 1993 and December 1994. Edinburgh.

Evaluation Strategy Working Group, September 1990.

Information Systems Strategy: Strategy Statement of SWSG. SWSG July 1993.

McAra, L. (1998) *Social Work and Criminal Justice: Early Arrangements*. Edinburgh: The Stationery Office.

McAra, L. (1998a) *Social Work and Criminal Justice: Parole Board Decision Making*. Edinburgh: The Stationery Office.

McIvor, G. and Barry, M. (1998) *Social Work and Criminal Justice: Probation*. Edinburgh: The Stationery Office.

McIvor, G. and Barry, M. (1998a) *Social Work and Criminal Justice: Community Based Throughcare*. Edinburgh: The Stationery Office.

Paterson, F. and Tombs, J. (1998) *Social Work and Criminal Justice: The Impact of Policy*. Edinburgh: The Stationery Office.

Social Work Services Group (1991) *National Objectives and Standards for Social Work Services in the Criminal Justice System*. Edinburgh: The Scottish Office.

Social Work Services Inspectorate for Scotland (1993). *National Inspection of Prison Based Social Work Units.* Edinburgh.

SPS/SWSG (1989). *Continuity Through Co-operation: A National Framework of Policy and Practice Guidance for Social Work in Scottish Penal Establishments*. Edinburgh: The Scottish Prison Service and Social Work Services Group.

SWSG/COSLA Joint Working Group: National Core Data System for Social Work Services in the Criminal Justice System. Minutes of meetings held in 1992.

The Main Consultation Group on Social Work Services in the Criminal Justice System. Minutes of meetings held in 1992, 1993 and 1995. Unpublished.

Working Group on the Review of National Standards for Throughcare. Minutes of May 1994 meeting. Unpublished.

Printed in Scotland for The Stationery Office Limited
J37711, C5, 2/98, CCN 003808

THE SCOTTISH OFFICE CENTRAL RESEARCH UNIT

Social Work Research Findings No. 15

Social Work and Criminal Justice: The National and Local Context

Louise Brown, Liz Levy, Gill McIvor

National Objectives and Standards for Social Work Services in the Criminal Justice System and the 100% funding initiative ('the policy') were introduced in 1991[1] in order to secure the provision of services which have the confidence of both criminal justice decision-makers and the wider public. This study is part of the social research programme designed to evaluate policy implementation. It sets the national and local context within which the other studies in the programme examine progress towards policy objectives.

Main findings

- National consultation, through the Main Consultation Group, and the planning process were found to have engendered a sense of ownership of service and policy objectives amongst key stakeholders.
- Initial planning procedures, problems in establishing national and local management information systems and the uncertainty of levels of funding, hindered local strategic planning. Social work managers believed that the development of a comprehensive approach to planning and service delivery was hindered by the fact that not all services were 100% funded.
- Managers in authorities with the clearest specialist structures believed that they had introduced more structured offence-focused methods of probation work.
- Respondents considered that throughcare was the area in which least progress had been made, partly because it was resource intensive, numbers were low and prison social work services were funded separately from community-based services.
- The Main Consultation Group did not facilitate effective monitoring or review of policy implementation. Interviewees identified a need for the establishment of a group to undertake this role.

1 National Standards for Community Service had been introduced in 1989.

1998

Introduction

The National Objectives and Standards (the Standards, 1991) set out a framework within which local authorities are required to provide social work services where costs are met by the 100 per cent funding initiative (initially social enquiry reports and associated court services, community service, probation, parole and other aspects of throughcare).

Prior to the development of the Standards, local authorities had to fund most social work services out of their general income. Criminal justice services were, therefore, in competition for resources with other local authority services and as a result were not always of sufficient quantity and quality to meet the requirements of the courts.

The main aims of the policy are:

- to reduce the use of custody by increasing the availability, improving the quality and targeting the use of community-based court disposals on those most at risk of custody, especially young offenders;
- to enable offenders to address their offending behaviour and make a successful adjustment to law-abiding life.

The purpose of this study was to describe the national and local context within which the policy had been developed, implemented and reviewed prior to and during the period in which the research programme was conducted.

Four social work authorities were selected for study, to reflect areas with urban centres, those which were predominantly rural and to represent both specialist and more generic forms of organising social work criminal justice services.

Findings are based on an analysis of central and local government policy and planning documents, and interviews in spring 1995 with: five members of the Main Consultation Group on Social Work Services in the Criminal Justice System; twelve social work managers and seven independent sector service providers located in the study areas.

Consultation

The Main Consultation Group was established in 1989 with the specific remit to review social work criminal justice services and to oversee production of the National Standards. Respondents considered that the Group had been most successful in involving key stakeholders in developing and generating a sense of corporate ownership of the National Standards.

Formal liaison, in which the judiciary were consulted about the quality and quantity of services and proposed developments, did not always take place in the study areas. However informal liaison between the judiciary and court social workers was found to operate well.

In some cases it was considered that liaison between the Scottish Prison Service and social work services, and between community-based social workers and those in prisons, could have been more effective.

Planning

Interviewees considered that local planning was hindered by: the initial planning procedures; the uncertainty of whether proposals in draft plans would receive financial support; problems in establishing national and local management information systems; and the delay in publication of Scottish Office criminal justice statistics and results of the Social Work Services Inspectorate's inspections of local services.

Revised planning procedures and the review of the National Core Data System were introduced to facilitate local planning in the future.

The Standards were believed to have encouraged the involvement of the independent sector in the planning process and facilitated good liaison arrangements which resulted in greater accountability.

The different funding mechanism of prison-based social work was considered to have had an adverse impact on the creation of an integrated throughcare service.

Service provision

Rural areas were said to have difficulties in accessing or providing services partly because of the relatively low demand and the reluctance of offenders to attend services outwith their local environment. This may have implications for the more rural new authorities.

The authorities in which the greatest progress had been made in introducing more structured, offence focused methods of probation work were, managers believed, those which had the clearest specialist structures.

Review of policy implementation

The Main Consultation Group was not seen to be effective in monitoring and reviewing policy implementation because it met on an annual basis and because (at the time of the research) there was a lack of a comparative national statistical information. Some Main Consultation Group members suggested that, in order to provide a strategic overview of policy implementation, a group such as the Main Consultation Group should be reconvened to encompass more focused representation of key groups and should meet more frequently.

Conclusion

The main factors which facilitated policy implementation included:

- the involvement of key stakeholders in the preparation of the National Standards;
- protected funding for core services;
- increase in practitioners' skills as a result of greater specialisation;
- planning, which provided a focus for development and the establishment of priorities;

The main factors which were seen to have inhibited policy implementation included:

- the absence of 100% funding for all services;
- failure in the allocation of funding, to recognise the resource implications of undertaking effective work with high tariff offenders;
- the lack of comparative national statistical information on policy implementation.

The study was carried out by The Scottish Office Central Research Unit and the Social Work Research Centre as part of the programme of research to evaluate social work criminal justice policy. The research programme was conducted by The Scottish Office Central Research Unit in collaboration with the Social Work Research Centre at Stirling University and with Edinburgh University. It was funded by the Home Department of The Scottish Office.

Social Work and Criminal Justice Volume 3: 'The National and Local Context'; the report of the research programme summarised in this Research Findings is published by The Stationery Office. It may be purchased from The Stationery Office, price £13 per copy.

Reports of Individual Studies on this programme are also available:
Social Work and Criminal Justice Volume 1: 'The Impact of Policy'.
Social Work and Criminal Justice Volume 2: 'Early Arrangements'.
Social Work and Criminal Justice Volume 4: 'Sentencer Decision-Making'.
Social Work and Criminal Justice Volume 5: 'Parole Board Decision-Making'.
Social Work and Criminal Justice Volume 6: 'Probation'.
Social Work and Criminal Justice Volume 7: 'Community-Based Throughcare'.

Cheques should be made payable to The Stationery Office and addressed to:

The Stationery Office Ltd, Mail Order Department, 21 South Gyle Crescent, Edinburgh, EH12 9EB. Telephone: 0131-479-3141 or Fax 0131-479-3142.

The following Research Findings for other studies on this programme are also available:

Findings 13: 'The Impact of Policy'
Findings 14: 'Early Arrangements'.
Findings 16: 'Sentencer Decision-Making'.
Findings 17: 'Parole Board Decision-Making'.
Findings 18: 'Probation'.
Findings 19: 'Community-Based Throughcare'.

Research Findings may be photocopied, or further copies may be obtained from:

The Scottish Office Central Research Unit

Room 53

James Craig Walk

Edinburgh EH1 3BA

or

Telephone: 0131-244-5397

Fax: 0131-244-5393

Designed and produced on behalf of The Scottish Office by The Stationery Office J16005 1/98

ISBN 0-7480-6661-6